DRUM DREAM GIRL

How One Girl's Courage Changed Music

poem by
Margarita Engle

illustrations by
Rafael López

Houghton Mifflin Harcourt
Boston   New York

On an island of music
in a city of drumbeats
the drum dream girl
dreamed

of pounding tall conga drums
tapping small *bongó* drums
and boom boom booming
with long, loud sticks
on big, round, silvery
moon-bright *timbales.*

But everyone
on the island of music
in the city of drumbeats
believed that only boys
should play drums

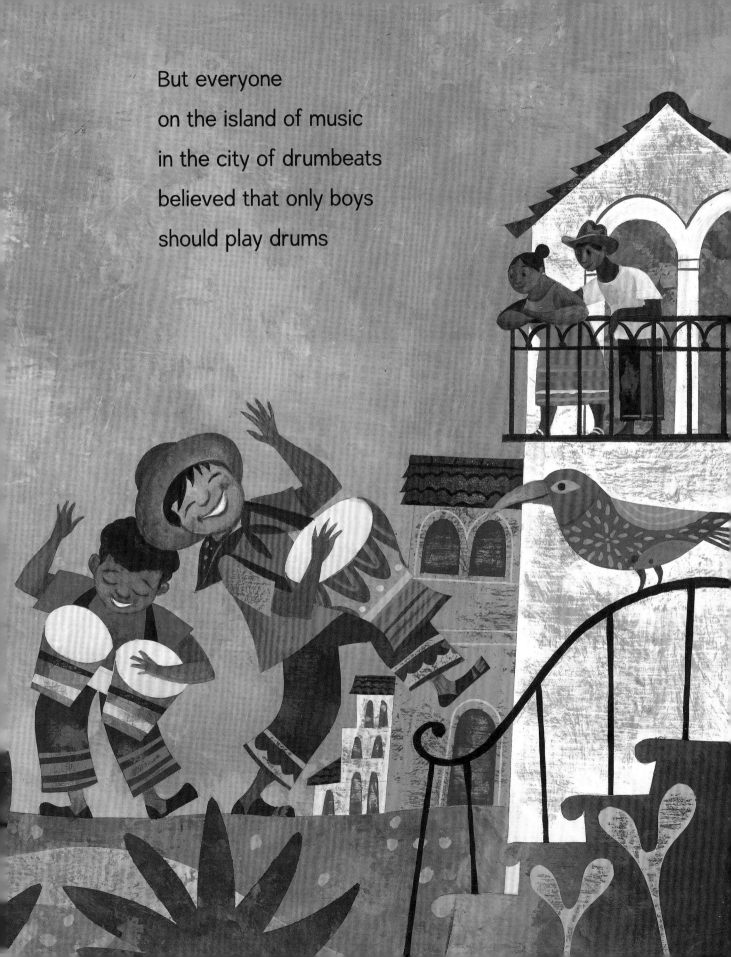

so the drum dream girl

had to keep dreaming

quiet

secret

drumbeat

dreams.

At outdoor cafés that looked like gardens
she heard drums played by men
but when she closed her eyes
she could also hear
her own imaginary
music.

When she walked under
wind-wavy palm trees
in a flower-bright park
she heard the whir of parrot wings
the clack of woodpecker beaks
the dancing tap
of her own footsteps
and the comforting pat
of her own
heartbeat.

At carnivals, she listened
to the rattling beat
of towering
dancers
on stilts

and the dragon clang
of costumed drummers
wearing huge masks.

At home, her fingertips
rolled out their own
dreamy drum rhythm
on tables and chairs . . .

and even though everyone
kept reminding her that girls
on the island of music
had never played drums

the brave drum dream girl

dared to play

tall conga drums

small *bongó* drums

and big, round, silvery

moon-bright *timbales*.

Her hands seemed to fly

as they rippled

rapped

and pounded

all the rhythms

of her drum dreams.

Her big sisters were so excited
that they invited her to join
their new all-girl dance band

but their father said only boys should play drums.

So the drum dream girl
had to keep dreaming
and drumming
alone

until finally
her father offered
to find a music teacher
who could decide if her drums
deserved
to be heard.

The drum dream girl's
teacher was amazed.
The girl knew so much
but he taught her more
and more
and more

and she practiced
and she practiced
and she practiced

until the teacher agreed
that she was ready
to play her small *bongó* drums
outdoors at a starlit café
that looked like a garden

where everyone who heard

her dream-bright music

sang

and danced

and decided

that girls should always

be allowed to play

drums

and both girls and boys

should feel free

to dream.

Historical Note

This poem was inspired by the childhood of a Chinese-African-Cuban girl who broke Cuba's traditional taboo against female drummers. In 1932, at the age of ten, Millo Castro Zaldarriaga performed with her older sisters as Anacaona, Cuba's first "all-girl dance band." Millo became a world-famous musician, playing alongside all the American jazz greats of the era. At age fifteen, she played her *bongó* drums at a New York birthday celebration for U.S. president Franklin Delano Roosevelt, where she was enthusiastically cheered by First Lady Eleanor Roosevelt. There are now many female drummers in Cuba. Thanks to Millo's courage, becoming a drummer is no longer an unattainable dream for girls on the island.

Acknowledgments

I thank God for creative dreams. I am indebted to the wonderful autobiography written by Millo's sister: *Anacaona: The Amazing Adventures of Cuba's First All-Girl Dance Band* by Alicia Castro, with Ingrid Kummels and Manfred Schäfer (Atlantic Books, London, 2002). Special thanks to my family, my editors Reka Simonsen and Jeannette Larson, designer Elizabeth Tardiff, and the entire HMH publishing team. —M.E.

Library of Congress Cataloging-in-Publication Data / Engle, Margarita. / The drum dream girl / by Margarita Engle ; illustrated by Rafael López. / pages cm / Summary: Illustrations and poetic text follow a girl in the 1920s as she strives to become a drummer, despite being continually reminded that only boys play the drums, and that there has never been a female drummer in Cuba. Includes note about Millo Castro Zaldarriaga, who inspired the story, and Anacaona, the all-girl dance band she formed with her sisters.
ISBN 978-0-544-10229-3 / [1. Drummers (Musicians)—Fiction. 2. Dance music—Fiction. 3. Sex role—Fiction. 4. Cuba—History—1909-1933—Fiction.] I. López, Rafael, 1961- illustrator. II. Title. / PZ8.3.E583Dru 2015 / [E]—dc23 / 2014015056

Manufactured in Italy · 23 · 4500840183

For my grandchildren —M.E.

For my architect mother, Pillo, whose courage opened
the ceiling above her dreams —R.L.